raw

sugar

a poetry collection
by

bri rader

raw sugar

bri rader

for eevee & holly,

may this book always be a reminder

to never give up

on yourself

raw sugar

bri rader

raw sugar

This is a work of creative nonfiction. Some parts have been

fictionalized in varying degrees, for various purposes.

First paperback edition May 2023

Book design by Bri Rader

ISBN 979-8-218-21751-8

with this book as my proof & my witness

it's raw sugar i have given you

the rest is up to your perceptions

(thank you for listening)

Words can speak just as loud as actions.

Words can hurt but they can also *heal.*

This book is a collection of thoughts and poems from
throughout my life.
They were all written about different experiences and
moments in time.
These poems reflect myself; my soul, and whatever
feelings transpire on entering,
I genuinely hope I connect with you, and give you a
friend that understands.
I will admit not every poem is a masterpiece but it is a
piece of me.

This book has the following depression, abuse,
addiction, rape, loss, and suicidal thoughts.

Reader discretion is advised. If you or someone you
know is suffering, it's never too late.

You are not alone.

You are worthy of saving.

You always were.

what is the difference between raw and refined sugar?

it's the process of removal of all the molasses from the
sugar crystals
by melting and filtering any impurities out. it is then
crystallized a
second time for the refined white sugar. white sugar
tends to be
sweeter than raw.

now, what is the difference between our true selves and
the self
we show others?

words
left unsaid
don't disappear
they just build

pressure

words have always been my escape
since i was young
when i can't convey
what i really want to say
i was so afraid
   to
     give them

raw sugar

i
put
refined
out on the table
hoping they would stay longer

(but do people who prefer refined over raw love sugar
or just want something sweet)

turn the clock sideways
nails from the carpet in the hallways
step with caution
your home is a foreign label
glass from lightbulbs on the table
hide underneath covers
screams and threats
still make their way to you
if they bleed, they will make you bleed too
smoke-stained outlines on the walls
from broken picture frames
if they are lonely, they will make you lonely too
use you as a pin cushion
for needles & thread to sew up their own wounds
instead
tie stones to your ankles and expected you **float**

(questioning what does it mean to be loved?)

trauma.

brainwashes us
it strips us of who we once were
till we are so overexposed
we shut down
like bleach in a sink
the smell is intoxicating
abuse is all we ever have known
so, it **becomes** normal
removing any part of us that is infected
the scalpel digs in deep
twist the knife
like i am under anesthetics
but i feel everything
tell me i am a nuisance
the meaning of my existence
is only for your **reassurance**
that you are in control

she wears a *yellow dress*
trying not to make a mess
she looks at the sky
hoping one day she could spread her wings
to take flight
somewhere she can feel at home
where her bruises won't follow
she constructed a world
all of her own
paper swans and endless fields of violets
crickets only chirp in harmony
her sorrow
keeps her caged
yearning to be free
the placebo she created
has been wearing off
the *yellow dress* becomes too tight
while she was busy forging what she
thinks the light feels like

she draws in chalk
little rainbows
shadows
from the overcast
closing in
her little rainbows
start to wash away
she realizes
they won't last
no matter how many
time she tries
little rainbows
become
smeared tears

i want to say so many things
but when it comes to it
i can't find the words to convey
circles in my head
i have been trying to convince myself
i am more than how you treated me
but these blackened waters keep pulling me under
the sharks can smell the blood from the lacerations
you didn't even bother to watch me drown
i am just the past you tried to erase
you are the pain i can't ever escape
my heart is suffocating
from overwhelming suffering
did you really ever care at all?
bloodstained hands you just rinse it off
like it was a disease
i am plunging into the deep
no one will come searching for me
only muscle memory keeps me breathing
these blackened waters have become

my comfort now

good girls do as they are told
good girls advertise what is sold
they don't tell secrets
sow our mouths shut
use our blood as holy water
verses turn into curses
paint the windows black
behind lock doors
my torture is your playground
good girls don't make a sound
in a world full of devils wearing human skin
they will shed it off under the covers
don't you know, *good girl?*
they will be there when you sleep
when you walk down the street
you can't escape their hold

showers

     can't erase

          everything

you have to exercise the demons out
they only prey on those who seem powerless
like a *snake to a mouse*
you don't have to accept being the victim
a snake might have venom
but we have the strength to overcome
the paralysis

to become the ones in control

this is my house
you aren't welcome
trying to move through the walls
insulation & copper wiring
but i will seal off every entry

*(i will be honest, pieces of you will die but that never
means your death)*

put your hands over my mouth
from being too loud
quiet
not a sound
no one can hear your cries
tears in my eyes
time moves so heavy
moments taking eternity
stolen things that cannot be returned
we cannot always
                    heal from being
                              burned

we have inherited
the weight & scars
from our
mothers & fathers
just like they did from theirs
passing down heirlooms of unresolved trauma
i was handed the torch
i will then look to my daughters
inner conversations turned
into realizations
i would rather
be consumed by the flame & smoke
than for them to know
the pain of being burned & choked

i have only ever known abusive love

this bruise reminds me
how toxic his love could be

but i just became reclusive
because i thought that was how love
was supposed to be

(i learned it from mother)

always searching for some form of acceptance

so i form a dependence
                        to your destructive ways
trying to find substance
                        in your wake
but all i found was pain

(i learned it from father)

the stars never really aligned for me
always on their own framework
shadows lurk
waiting for their moment
to overtake every little fragment of light
leaving me in the darkness
wrapping itself around me
and it's too comforting to

leave

bri rader

could i ever rebuild
from the destructive wake of you?

will I ever recover from your toxins?

i try to grab for the rest of the rope
but I begin to lose my grip
my sanity holding by threads
and i'm heading for the cliffs
all this weight i've been holding onto
is putting a strain on me
cutting off circulation
keep quiet no use of screaming out loud
no one will hear you
when you fall

coal burns on my feet
from walking barefoot
i was naive
to believe
you wouldn't hurt me

decompression sickness
sinking into your depths
forgetting to come back up for breaths
you lured me down into your abyss
decorated the illusion with rubies and pearls
the light you have shown me pretending to lead the way
to safety but you only wanted to feast on my innocence
and watch pieces of me rot away

i have been
falling
for some time
i fell right through the rails
trying to grasp
onto anything
with these broken fingernails
that is when i met you
dripping in cement
trying to cover your intent
you fed me pretty lies
just to try and
steal my life

i am afraid of letting you down
trying to make myself shine
like a firefly
only to get lost in the crowd
somehow in all the luminescence
you wanted my presence
i am afraid of losing you now
used to all those who come to walk out
like a conversation that has gone dry
only to wonder what it feels like not to bleed
from their daggers and bullets, they leave behind
somehow even though i am covered with wounds and
scars
you saw beauty in this heart
i never want this to

fade away

cosmic dust
surrounds us
on a collision course and
i'm set on you
everything we have been through
galaxies seem empty without you
do you think of me in the same light too?
shooting stars keep secrets
underneath the moon

i have been wishing to see you soon

in this translucent vibrance of lights
against our skin
twilight conversations fill the hours
a shimmer of daylight echoes onto these feelings
show me every color you don't display
we don't have to paint within this frame
let's go somewhere no one else goes
discover another point of view
we don't have to wait for a cue
i never want to lose this sight of you

i would have moved mountains
crossed dangerous seas
just to get a glimpse of your
luminescent properties
tell me,
all your dreams
let them take form
oh, how they shimmer
you wore
them all so beautifully
like a favorite scene from a movie
replaying in my head
irises
prance in the breeze so carefree
like they were in **love**
imprints in the grass from where we touched
strange
our bodies felt so light
they were levitating
you asked
"where i was headed next?"

i must confess
i want to follow **you**

we built our love on top
of fault lines
regardless
i wanted to explore your diamond mines

take my hand
don't let go
through the highs and lows
even if the words aren't wrapped with a bow
your touch on my bare skin
i don't care where you begin
kisses on my bedstand
stretch myself out
so you could fit inside my house
i spent my life waiting for the rain
to pour
you found
me out
in the dust storm
you took my hand
didn't know it was you that
i have been searching for
you're melting in my mouth
like sugar

(read the words in bold separately.)

you seemed so safe
like a fortress
i wanted to let myself disappear in you
your design
was flawless
your body was lawless
how could I not

                  see the cracks in your seams?

surround
yourself in moonlight
you never once showing
your insecurity
unearthing myself
hoping you would have taken me with you
roots exposed
to the harsh sunlight
as i start to wilt
you show no guilt
was it all
just imaginary?

little fragments
lay at our feet
hoping they will meet
in the same way
splinters on my fingers
trying to put them back in place
all i end up doing is making myself bleed
retrace my reflection
knowing i can't erase imperfections
but i am *starting to forget how they went*

words unsaid
surrounding us like vultures
the things we tried to ignore are on a
collision course
we aren't fighting just to keep score
any more
silence fills the void with acidic thoughts
eating away at what is left
lying to ourselves again
that
nothing is
wrong

raw sugar

i would carry you through the storm
even if you are worn
i think you are ethereal
shall anyone would try to lay harm on you
i would protect you
like a knight to a king
put my life on the line to give you peace of mind
no one could outshine your display
even if you think you have become dull
i think you are beautiful
shadows try to dance and put you in a trance
i would cast them away
like a hero in a play
i would give you everything
like a mother to her son
never shunning you away
even if you wouldn't do the same

you're killing me slowly
wondering what i am doing wrong
suffocating myself with laces
on nights i spent laying alone
wondering why you don't love
in the way i need you too
you have a hold on me
too tempting so sweet
yet when i bite down it's bitter to me
why can't you love me like you love her?
could i ever be all you adore and more?
tell me, i can't take the lies you have been feeding me
you're killing me slowly
wondering if i am enough
to spend hours in the mirror trying to convince myself
you don't love in
the way i need

somewhere along the way
we lost sight of what we ever aiming for to begin with
like a distant dream we can't quite place but
didn't all the way erase
the faint lines still remain

your twisted intent
masqueraded by sweet words
your sharpened blade
camouflaged by roses
you'll watch me bleed out
while you act innocent
this game you've been playing
while i kept begging for any sign of love
is coming to an end

empty words fill my head with gasoline
i've built this house on the foundation of you
and
with every lie, you tell me
it's like matches
catching fire to the vapors in the air
lingering over me like anxiety
it's suffocating
i can't breathe as flames engulf everything
my hands are burning from trying to salvage
us
as you stand there to watch it all burn

when someone you once loved
becomes a stranger
when someone you would die for
becomes the enemy
when someone you promised the world
is no longer in yours

staring at each other
at these crossroads
where do you go where i cannot follow?
my life without you has become hollow
do our memories not mean anything?
all those promises we shared did they not have any
substance?
this distance between us has become so vast
i've been chasing you even if it's an illusion of who you
used to be
our hearts are such fragile things
cannot accept the absence of the things we haven't
come to terms with
could we ever be what we were again?
without any warning, you keep your goodbyes dry
tell me,
when did all this slip through our hands?

why doesn't anything ever last?

your blade in my back
not quite sure how long i've been bleeding
i gave you my best but i guess
you didn't notice that
my eyes water trying to wake up from this dream
i only found myself drifting out to sea
sinking further down
i wish i could have taken flight with you
but i have been fighting the current over my head all
this time
you were a sight to behold
but now you're just a story to be told
when i try to remember how the sky looked with you
now it is nothing but different shades of blue

i want an escape
from my rotting existence
words sitting on the surface of
my racing mind
i don't know what i expected to find
on the outside, i wanted flowers but got weeds
i need a way out of here
from this dark room
but the light is just as lonely
sugar from your hand as you offer salvation
but all i taste is salt
i know it's my fault
as we stand here
but i can't live another moment
trapped in this place
the hands of time reach out to me
but they are too short to touch

falling,
        falling

can i ever go back?

put my heart in a blender
guess i wanted to pretend
a while longer
painted smiles say "i'm fine"
but on the inside
my skin starts to feel like cracking ice
getting too attached was always my vice
my greatest fear is the end
so i drag things on instead
my hold starts to slip so i spin out
crashing into my stability
causing my composure to rupture

(i always pretended to have such great structure)

raw sugar

long drives
you're on my mind
on repeat
the stars would look brighter with you here
you call, i'll always answer
push me away,
i'll just keep on admiring you
you speak those sweet words
like honey in my tea
but then you go and leave me
like a cool breeze in july
where do you go, darling?
cause my mind always wanders back to you

am i just a passing stranger?
well, you're just another scar that i cover up in the
mirror
i go out trying to drink you out of my mind
but i just find
myself wanting you more each time
i know i am not even in your search history
my misery drips from my face like
wax from a candle on a blacked-out night
wishing i could find an escape
but i am stuck in one place
can't seem to ever get high enough to never come back
down
i need to drown you out
burning every memory let the flames consume them
now
the wound is still fresh
i can't seem to let the flesh close
now it's infected from reminiscing about us
about
what was,
> *what could have been,*
>> and what we have

become

say it under your breath
maybe it's better this way
we burned out before we even got to glow
it goes to show
that there are some things we can't control
no use in apologizing
we weren't meant to be
we let ourselves go
separate ways
now it's just another day without you
sometimes things we let go of
never come back

you linger throughout my mind
underneath my floral print sheets
i wish you could be right here
with me
but instead,
you sleep underneath a different sky
than me
i've been going through the motions
but i'll always be the ocean trying to touch the moon
gravity always manages to bring me back down too
soon
i dream of a day we could be everything we promised
but that's not how
this
story
ends

compression from your impression
leaving me with depression
every corner of my mind
is the only place you decided to stay
always looking behind
waiting for you to be there
but your footprints faded   a w a y

i have learned how to get burned
i have learned that no one else can mend these wounds
healing doesn't come as easy as misery
ripped my wings off before i could ever take flight
closed the blinds when it was light
when i look into the mirror i want to see something
worthy
giving when all they ever do is take
i had to try and fill myself of the void
you had left behind
i want to find meaning in the ruins you had made me

i have put aside
parts of myself i try to hide
they don't get to see the light
put them away in a drawer with letters addressed to you
never to have them in view
she never stood a chance
only craved to be seen in perfect lighting
but you always glance right through
my hand trembling reaches out
the darkness covers me
would I rather be lonely than feel anything?

what is a flower to a butterfly?
gives passionate kisses
then just leaves
like it didn't mean anything at all
the flower will be in awe
as it watches it fly away
hoping they meet again *someday*

i told myself this is the last time
but i keep giving in to you
a little to top off your lonely evening
but it stings
my heart yearns to be loved by you
a little to top off my lonely evening
but you never stay just long enough to
make me strung out over the thought of you
i have been flipping over rocks trying to find
an answer key on quitting this one-sided affair
but I come up empty tossing pennies into thin air
waiting till *midnight*
to get another dose
even if it makes me go *comatose*

surrendering
        myself
to temptation
        conversations
running rampant
        between you & me
like a moth to a flame
        it's useless to fight
because we both know i'll give in
        every time
even if i burn
        could i ever learn
to stay away
        from you?

we may have never met
but i loved you
we may have never touched
but i held you
one day we will find each other
in a field of daffodils
you will take my hand
we will play till the sun melts away
swings and climbing trees
we could pretend to touch the sky
not a day goes by
i don't think about your life
and what you might have been like
these tears fall and
i somehow feel you catch them all
no name is written on stone
no pictures on the wall
but i will always remember
your *precious soul*

bri rader

i have traveled far
to follow that spark in the dark
but that beacon was your heart
that guided me
across murky waters
don't close the door on me
leaving me out in the cold
i don't want to go on wondering
how you feel next to me
lifetimes i would have waited to see your face
in the morning light
not a penny to our names
but i don't need any fortune or fame
just you and me
on this open road
always had the problem of racing to the finish line
when i wished i would have taken my time and
held onto moments before they grew old
don't want us to be some dust-covered story
that will go untold

secrets that get hung up on the wires
their whispers never tire
pretend that they don't exist
but they will always manage to resurface
they twist, bend, and contour themselves to things that
won't mend

i have been here before
maybe in a dream, i can't quite place
your face looks so divine in these fluorescent lights
i don't want this night to come to an end
because maybe by morning you will disappear
please baby tell me you will still be here

even if it's not true

our loneliness met in the middle
where we burnt so hot it melted
like lightning on a summer's night
we danced like it was our last
now your kisses feel foreign
you keep walking out the door
tell me,
you'll be back
i wish you wouldn't go
and leave me
alone

the lustrous stars
paint the twilight
in radiant hues
but nothing compares to you

swimming pools
with hidden jewels
i want to dive into that cool blue
seeing how long i can hold my breath
like a child
just to try and hold a piece of your light
the coarse bottom may be rough
against my bare skin
but
how this sun reflects on you
like an aurora across the vermiculite
it's more than enough
for me to try and get a better view

of you

through these vines
i found you and
on this balcony,
we performed alchemy
mixture of
serotonin & dopamine
creating an elixir
if this is just a temporary cure
i won't mind the overexposure
luscious magnolia lingers in the air
your fingers weaving through my hair

i only want one more dance
while we have the chance

i have been stranger
to myself
balancing above rouge waves
do you believe in fate,
or do you play it safe?

(i am trying to play for keeps)

bri rader

been wandering around the universe
touching stardust
searching for something unknown
amongst the cosmic display
i fall into orbit
caught in your gravity
crash landed into you

your intoxicating hints of *lavender mint*
is too strong for me to resist
two lonely strangers float on like clouds
just trying to feel something
but can never quite hold onto anything
this world is so full yet so vacant
transparent souls found
each other in the tiny folds
where the need for each other overflows
and lavender mint grows
you have me coming undone at the seams
like it was a dream
but we just phase right through
tell me can we pretend
we could be whole again

i always bloom too soon
like a
forthysia
i try to greet you with
pale primrose yellow flowers
from this rigid winter's grasps
if you even noticed my petals won't last
only attracting the wasps & nats
what is lost
perhaps was never mine, to begin with,
i still
romanticize
in my spare time
how it would feel if
you would admire me
even after springtime
has past

(i always fall in love too quickly)

raw sugar

couldn't avoid
damage from the embers

blistering
        from
                burns
                        you left on me

my sense of direction is destroyed

where
        do i
                go
                        when you're not with me?

bri rader

chasing after the taste
of sweet adrenaline
droplets of chlorine off my fingertips
with hints of vodka
driving down the interstate
going at least over a hundred
didn't pay enough attention
to the shutter speed
recall the number of light poles?
they all are just a blur
you are out with her
under this champagne moonlight
while i am role-playing with devils

does she unravel
             her laces for you?

in the way i use to?

raw sugar

whispers down the hall
from ghosts that won't exercise
themselves from you
lingering the air has gone stale
and it's getting harder to breathe
it all in anymore
i only wanted to be close to you
but no matter how much i say it's not true
you don't love me, in the same way,
please tell me
it's in your silence that i hear it the most
you can lie through your teeth but i see right through
this disguise you put on display
is it me that you dream of or am i just a temporary fix
for
a damaged heartbreak?

bri rader

when will you
beg me to stay?
when will you
walk away and look back

because you can't leave as easily?
when will you love me
the same way?
i could only hope for an answer
standing here, with memories you have taken
that i never wished for
you had me, underneath
drowning in my own insecurities
now you left and gave me room to breathe
you could have had me

not like if we were to catch up, we could make up
for lost time
the second hand stole all my seconds
spent it spinning in circles
not like if we were to catch up we could try to
rewind them

these memories of you
i can't seem to let go
keeps me attached to you
even when you cut the threads that tie me to you
i only got tangled in the loose strings
the more
      i struggled
           the more
               knotted
                  i became

expose yourself for a one-time use antidote for
loneliness
let them all adore your laces and done-up faces
you never ever really show what's it all for
you're just another score on their tally board
they all want to get a glimpse for their one-time use
you just want to feel something real but you'll never get
that in an online preview
you become lost in a crowd of plastic roses and risqué
poses
you never really show what's it all for
pour yourself out to make more room for the right angle
of you
erase your name for a moment of fame
your dreams are just another nail in the telephone poll

silly girl,
don't you know they don't want to see your heart
silly girl,
they never wanted to talk about your dreams from the
start
you thought those false words masquerade with
sweetness
was true
staring into the rearview mirror trying to understand
but it was in between the lines, the fine print,
you misread what they were selling to you
you wanted some affection, they just wanted some self-
satisfaction
you just happen to be the one-use tissue for their lonely
night regime
silly girl,
when will you learn that they will take what they want
and leave you
silly girl,
you fell in love with a thief
in a kingdom of sheep
now you lay as you weep
while you are leaking what is left of your core
all over the floor

you discarded me
because you
didn't want to make room in your life
i was
the calamity
the sacrifice
you spit lies in the mirror to make yourself feel better
are you satisfied with your disaster?
pull back your layers and you'll find your answer
guilty, guilty the whispers become even clearer
you will never admit the truth
because that would make you look inferior
now you write "I love you" on letters
you may have given me my name
but you will always be a **stranger**

(my forgiveness is not a handout, but a treasure and you
don't deserve either)

i have been trapped in this carousel
i could never tell
what you were thinking
trying to get off
i fell
and scraped my knees
i could never tell
what you wanted from me

you have me in chains
around my neck
pull me in tighter
i'll beg for more
whatever you have in store
it's everything i adore
left me thirstier than ever before
craving your skin on mine
can we meet one more time?
i know you're not good for me
but i want to taste the tainted side
distractions is all we really need
to get by
like *morphine*
numbing myself from

                             anything

where do i begin?
it starts where she ends
the thread from her seams
unraveled
trying desperately to fill herself
from things they have stolen
all the pieces lay broken
could they ever be whole again?

raw sugar

unfiltered cinders
find her
scar tissue so deep
it won't heal properly
the dragon's keep
is where she wondered
stench of sulfur fumes
counteracts her vanilla perfume

little did she know this would be her doom

this darkness is everlasting
i move forward even if the end is untouchable
your smile is all i need to find hope for a new tomorrow
my heart is bruised and malfunctioning but you still
find
beauty in this sorrow

my self-destructive tendencies
always manages
to catch backup

with me

where do you go, when i am lonely?
should i believe the lies you told me?
like a ticking timebomb one wrong wire away from an
explosion,
this inescapable pressure weighs us down
like an ocean current sweeping us underneath
these crashing waves show no remorse
do we really let things take their course?

raw sugar

> i am beyond repair
> been teetering on the brink of despair
> rather be alone than get too close

why is it we always push away those who love us most?

fallen through the erosion
corrosion
has taken its course
over us
how can i reach you
when this distance is just an expanding force
we can seem to break free of?
                dishwater starts to become lakes
                    water overflows from the sink
this never-ending
silence
between us has slowly taken its hold
sank its claws so deep it's rooted in our bones
your face grows cold
my flesh is exposed
                    floorboards start to mold
how can i fix the things i cannot erase
when you threw away the paper in the first place?

(communication is a dying art i never could master it)

bouquets of flowers
lose their luster
clusters of stars
lose their will to shine
time we took for granted
spills out
and it evaporated
before we noticed
pictures get creases
from being tossed around
loose ends become forgotten
like
dried flowers
didn't make a sound
as they fell to the *ground*

an ode to you

galaxies hide in your eyes
never knowing
what is on your mind
you distance yourself

we walk along the shoreline
i want to cipher
what you're after
you won't show me your rosetta stone

all i wanted was for you
to want me in the same light
i hold on tight
but it's past its prime

time to let you go.

(i have loved you in all your forms
why can't you love me in all mine?)

transparent
even in a full room
just passing faces traveling through

connections
only become failed interactions

stuck on thoughts
like walking on train tracks
they never truly have an end
what am i trying to defend?

(if i couldn't even protect you)

bri rader

soldering copper & iron
tying knots in cables
wires
exposed through its insulation
sketching maps out of constellations
but they are shy
disappearing without warning
trying to find my way
out at sea
through thin & uncertainty

how long have i been the villain
in this play?
was i always the hurricane
causing destruction in my wake?
mistake your silence
as your final answer
if i am a demon then you're the caster
plaster on the walls to cover holes
over things we can't control
like oil to water
all we do is cause a chemical fire

(we were no good for each other)

dead ends
disguising themselves as exits
with its
sequins on mannequins in the window display
replacing my sorrow with receipts
chiffon & leather
making me feel complete
like morning coffee with a shot of expresso
add a caramel drizzle it will match my jewels
cat's eye & garnet
i spent so i don't have to admit
i was thrown off balance by you
so
accessories become a homemade remedy
for heartache

*(if i am going to carry baggage i want it to be
decorated)*

i'm addicted to the euphoria of falling in love
infatuated with the process of metamorphosis
our hearts coming out of their chrysalis
it doesn't have to make sense
as long as we are in each other's presence
becoming a butterfly before you
will the wind blow me away to where you couldn't
catch up?

if your gonna grab me first put on your gloves
even gold and silver tarnishes over time
between the sulfur and moisture
even clear waters become
cloudy after a rainstorm so i head back to shore

you ask
"what are you after?"

i'm
always chasing that euphoria

ohio october skies
tinted burnt orange sunsets
kaleidoscope of changing leaves
do they too have any regrets?

or

do they just

die?

(do they even question why?)

what animal best represents your soul?

i am an **eel.**

once i have bitten down
i cannot be removed without decapitation
like a wax seal
but
my toxins will cause an infection
rotting your flesh
wishing we had never met

i don't feel
there is nothing left
among the crevices of rocks in the reef
where i linger
i am not bitter
i just don't show any affection
or emotion
besides the fake smile i always wear
it's the way i am wired, it's how i survived
so distant
you'll wonder what i am thinking
i won't share
because i have figured it out for so long without anyone
there
but deep down
i want to know how it feels to let someone in
to feel love
and to show it as well

your name
like shackles and chains around me
saying it out loud is almost forbidden
leaving a sour taste in my mouth
i try to rinse it out
but only blood from my tongue stains the sink
i hate to think
you held me just to cause me pain
said my name just to throw it away
what a waste you have became
hidden yourself among the lies you have done
your name used to excite me
now it's just feels wrong

to say out loud

i can't wait to speak with you
i open my mouth but no words come out
maybe it's better that way
if i say nothing let you walk away
thinking i haven't missed you at all
i know this is getting old
and stale
but i have fallen through the rails
i tried to catch myself with broken fingernails
and bruised wrists becoming numb
i slowly lose my grip from you
you don't have a clue as you continue to enjoy the view
how could i blame you when i got too close
please don't search for me
i know you won't find a body
words bled out unable to reach you
these words will
never reach you
i know you won't look long for me
if at all
so it's better for me to say nothing
just letting you walk away thinking
i never loved you at all

i was covered in dirt before
i learned how to grow
i let myself take all the abuse
in fear of losing you
countless bruises, endless excuses for your bloody
knuckles
you tried to bury me alive
wanted me to struggle underneath all the rubble
of your unsolved issues

but even through concrete cracks
flowers can

bloom

i want to get to know your every desire
make them ignite like fire
set the world ablaze
with every vision you have, into a reality, i will make
make no mistake
i want to drown in your sins
and let it overtake me slowly, i want to savor
every drop
every time you smile i cave in, can't resist it
just want your poisonous kiss to infect my core
and i will be begging
for more

i sabotage things when it's perfect
just can't be content
i have to take it all out of context
convinced i am better off alone
never could drive in a straight line
you ask what's wrong i'll always respond with
"i'm fine"
i've been wearing faces to deal with different phases
these demons i've been avoiding
have been making a mess out of my head

they say when you get older, you'll understand
we are a prisoner of time
i didn't get the message till i found myself trying to
catch up
with seconds that pass on by
carelessly we let it slip through our hands
repeating all the moments we cannot get back
getting stuck in the past like quicksand
my grip on the present getting further and further away
as the future starts to play
all those pictures around us get dusty
open that window
let it air out
the moment is waiting for you
if you wait too long it

will pass on

a sky with wrinkle blue
a dash of periwinkle too
somehow looks different without you
you were with me through all my lows
and rose me higher than before
no matter what road i took you were
there beside me
all those memories we shared i will cherish even
when you go
somewhere i can't quite yet follow
when i was lonely you comforted me
wiped away all my tears
i know you want me to be happy
you left me in a good place
wishing you could enjoy it with me
i know your life here has come to an end
but you will always be here to watch me grow
to see what adventures i have ahead
so walk with me, my friend
till we meet again

(i wish i could have saved you)

this slow dance has grown tiresome
it was my favorite song
but the record has spun so much
it's lost its special touch
everyone else has gone home
and here we are awkwardly standing
in the middle of the stage

balloons will lose their helium
all fires burn themselves out
that adhesive that kept us together
starts to lose its grip now

where does that leave us at the end of everything?

near the creek
where the wild violets bloom,
i sit and stare into the abyss
where the memories flood
overtake my body
sweep me off my feet
into realms of dreams
where reality won't find me
where we could have stayed for eternity
you just left me missing who you used to be
the light peek-a-boos from the trees
but it doesn't give me the clarity i need
those nights when you wanted me to lay beside you
comes to an end
your gaze hasn't matched mine lately
was i just a fool to believe time couldn't claim us too?
maybe

but only for *you*

raw sugar

i was caught up in the display
decorated with city lights like tapestries
we didn't care where this would lead
impulsive but we were free
never a second thought to fall into you
you promised you would never go astray from me
we'd run through sprinklers at midnight
you said we would be forever
now the sunsets against the window screen

where do you go when you are lonely?
cuts and bruises all over
honey and sugar taste the dishonesty in the air
you wonder will they even care?
you are reaching the bottom of despair
now you are seeking the daylight
while you are sinking deeper
how long have you been fighting these monsters in
your head?
asking yourself if you are better off dead
like a *butterfly caught in a rainstorm*
you push through instead
in hopes that a rainbow
                              will lie at the
                                        end

these feelings start to decay
we let them all slip away
knives at our throats
should have known better than to get too close
i would have bled out for you
never thought it would be you to cut me down
your masqueraded lies
covered in silk reveals you have been scheming
this entire time
i have been caught up in dreaming
to notice your signs
conspiring my demise
all the promises
you gave
         dried out
they mean nothing now

bri rader

creating mosaics from shrapnel & eroded enamel

untangle myself from snares & nightmares

threads from tears become suede fringe & velvet tassels

the night grows late & i drew an ace of spades

wading through this crystal ball made of quarts,
amethyst, or glass

basking in the moonlight & neon signs

whiskey on the rocks & promises that won't last

i wish for the best

but wishes become pocket change & spent on cheap
cigarettes

in the shoe box
stored in the closet
where i keep lockets of
memories with you
empty perfume bottles
line up perfectly
on the window sill
handwritten notes we kept in our pockets
laces from our shoes tied together
tickets for the county fair
cotton candy kisses on the ferris wheel
baby we promised forever
like fools
and now your just
in a shoe box
stored in my closet

all those promises we tell ourselves

sell us out

all those questions are demanding **answers**

(what do I tell them?)

we use our words like daggers
carelessly throwing them at each other
no matter how you try to treat the wounds
it will always

scar

you have become entrapped
in my thorns
enticed from my blooms
tell me you don't want me
but i know you think of me
alone in your room
but i won't pretend your attention
is not my
addiction

your silence is screaming
volumes
these rooms are dark
you haven't even bothered to turn on **the** light
all those thoughts you tried to push back in your mind
keeps emerging
you'll submerge **right** into them
trying to see a way out it becomes like
a faint dream
you want to succumb to what has made you numb
just waiting to disappear,
the **answers** are so unclear
how to win against all the things you fear
laying there
almost given up
on yourself
finger on the *trigger*
the barrel **is** cold
the air gets heavier
you can't breathe under the pressure
then you hear a voice call out
from the *surface*

"Don't do it, darling"

"there is too much left to be done"
(repeat the words in bold as many times as you need)

smile
even when i wanted to
take my own life moments before
you walked in the door
words become like hail
razors don't cut deep enough
anymore
trying to hold someone's hand but
i feel so out of reach
waiting for someone to breach the sea
to get to me
been alone on this beach for some time
so i decided to
turn sand into castles
and tally marks into *words*

like a lighthouse to ships
i have found my life purpose

with these words

(i have found self-worth)

recovery is a journey
to sew the mind and soul
together once again
regaining control
over yourself
realizing the right things
to let go of
recognizing you are worthy
of happiness
and becoming
renewed

(it's the five r's of revelation)

i have had dreams like this
where you gave me a kiss underneath the
starlight
this sight is something new
never once was scared of falling with you
reaching for these escaping seconds
as they slip between my fingers
never really thought to count in between the lines
but right now, i want to cherish them all with you
i've been waiting all this time
for someone to show me a brand-new view
when the world is in shades of gray you shown
me a vibrate hue of blue

you aren't mine

i am not yours

we don't belong

does that make this wrong?

maybe

why does that turn me on?

say my name

i'll collapse

   &

i'll relapse

back to you

*(if you can't have something, you want it even more
until the desire is so great, you risk everything to obtain
it)*

a wolf cloaked in sheep's clothing
will admit nothing
blood dripping from their mouth
it is you they will devour
yet they will complain about the taste being too sour

bri rader

you want me to cover my skin

to help you hide
your demons within

("look at how she's dressed"
is an excuse for monsters to prey on the loose
without tying the knot on the noose)

you are so delicate
in every aspect
i hope i won't be another regret

golden thunderbolts dance across the sky

clouds molt themselves into turquoise tears they cry

your aesthetic is magnetic

as the voltage intensifies

ignoring all the signs to steer clear

from your storm

firmly i navigate straight forward

till i arrive to where you are

ignite my dormant soul
with your paper and coal

(we will catch fire together)

i have made diamonds out of lemons

*(you have the strength to overcome anything you put
your mind too & then some)*

i gave off so much light
that i became blind
and i thought
i was in the darkness
this whole time

if they didn't want you with lemons, they don't deserve
your diamonds

(you have always been a gift from nature)

i've laid it down
no matter what you think
bitter or sweet,
it's still **sugar**
i'll keep
being me
while you
watch me become the ruler
of my own kingdom
watch me obtain freedom & gain the reason
to be comfortable in my own skin
the rain has washed away the dirt from being buried
underneath all this construction
i've carried all this weight for way to long

oh, hello
how are you? it's been ages since we have talked

reflections of myself through the cracks in the
infrastructure
it was so tiresome staring at mirrors & out of windows
i have accepted where there is sun, there will be
shadows
the water is unclear but you won't know what you'll
find until you dive in
i am no longer *refined*
but
raw

bri rader

you have read my words,
                        these sentences carry so much

so i don't to carry all the burden

in the end

all you have

is your words

it is a gift yet a curse

it is our choices that decide their use & their purpose

**about
the
author**

Bri Rader was born in 1995 in Oceanside, California. Adopted by a
family in Cincinnati, Ohio at the age of 4. She attends Bellevue
University in Graphic Design BSD. She has always excelled in
literature, especially in creative writing. She uses poetry as a form of
expression and an outlet. She enjoys nature, especially insects and
flowers.

www.ingramcontent.com/pod-product-compliance
Lightning Source LLC
Chambersburg PA
CBHW060328050426
42449CB00011B/2692